C000130798

Successfully Going Freelance in a week

BRIAN HOLMES

Hodder & Stoughton

A MEMBER OF THE HODDER HEADLINE GROUP

Acknowledgements

For Mel, for her support and belief in me.

I would also like to thank not only all my friends who helped me when I started up as a freelancer, but also the following who have spent their time and energy in reading and commenting on the drafts of this book: David, Karen, Isobel, John and Mike.

Order queries: please contact Bookpoint Ltd, 39 Milton Park, Abingdon, Oxon OX14 4TD. Telephone: (44) 01235 400414, Fax: (44) 01235 400454. Lines are open from 9.00 - 6.00, Monday to Saturday, with a 24 hour message answering service. Email address: orders@bookpoint.co.uk

British Library Cataloguing in Publication Data
A catalogue record for this title is available from The British Library

ISBN 0 340 71204 X

First published 1996
Second edition 1998

Impression number	10	9	8	7	6	5	4	3	2	1
Year	2002	2001	2000	1999	1998					

Typeset by Multiplex Techniques Ltd, St Mary Cray, Kent.
Printed in Great Britain for Hodder & Stoughton Educational, a division of Hodder Headline Plc, 338 Euston Road, London NW1 3BH by Cox and Wyman, Reading, Berkshire.

FOUNDATION

The Institute of Management (IM) exists to promote the development, exercise and recognition of professional management. The Institute embraces all levels of management from student to chief executive and supports its own Foundation which provides a unique portfolio of services for all managers, enabling them to develop skills and achieve management excellence.

For information on the various levels and benefits of membership, please contact:

Department HS
Institute of Management
Cottingham Road
Corby
Northants NN17 1TT
Tel: 01536 204222
Fax: 01536 201651

This series is commissioned by the Institute of Management Foundation.

C O N T E N T S

At some point in their working life, I suspect everybody dreams of doing their own thing – working for themselves. As you are reading this book, you are thinking the same thing: no more bosses, you can pay yourself as much as you want, and you don't have to work if you don't want to.

The current trends of *out-sourcing, tele-commuting* and *going portfolio*, with the emphasis on 'cyber-technology' and 'information wealth', only enhances the possibility. In fact, the trends are almost prophetic about the way in which the labour market will develop in the future. Whether these trends turn out to be true or not is largely irrelevant to this book; there have always been, and will always be, those who want to work by themselves, for themselves.

This book is written for those people who wish to go free-lance. Freelance is a term which has certain implications. It usually identifies those people with skills and experience that they can 'sell' to others. Such categories of people may be consultants (management, computer and others), designers, writers, financial advisers and many others. Freelancers are also likely to work as a 'one-man band'. This book is not primarily intended for people looking to set up small businesses, such as retail outlets, and manufacturing companies, although much of the book would be useful for those people.

There are five main questions to look at with regard to going freelance:

- Are you the right sort of person?
- Do you have the right skills to sustain a business?
- Do you have the relevant experience and contacts?
- What are the logistics of going freelance?
- How does it affect your life?

Over the next seven days, we will look at why you want to go freelance, what you have to do and how it will change your life.

Sunday	Going Freelance – an overview
Monday	The first steps
Tuesday	The financial side
Wednesday	Earning money
Thursday	Maintaining the work flow
Friday	Life matters
Saturday	The main points

Going freelance – an overview

Today we will look at the pros and cons of going freelance, why you want to go freelance and whether you are the right sort of person to go freelance. But first, what does 'freelance' mean?

What does freelance mean?

Being freelance essentially means being self-employed. This means that there is no boss – only yourself (and your customers) – and no strict rules and regulations of employment. On the other hand, there is no guaranteed work, and therefore no regular income.

There are three main ways of working for yourself: as an *individual*, in a *partnership* and as a *limited company*. Although the main focus of this book is on the individual way, a brief overview of the others is also important.

Individual
This is where one person decides to set up their own business, usually 'selling' their knowledge, skills and expertise. You are liable for damages and losses if a legal claim is successfully made against you, which could result in personal ruin, as you are liable for everything. The best way of remembering what it is to be freelance are the Inland Revenue's criteria for being self-employed. These are:

- You must have more than one client
- You must not work exclusively from one client's office, or exclusively use their equipment

Partnership

This is where two or more people decide to form a business with each other. The important aspect of partnerships is that you need to be able to work with and trust one another. It is recommended that a legal agreement be drawn up between the partners to protect each other's interests, including how to break the partnership if needed. Like an individual, you are both liable for any debts or claims against you. Also, you are liable for your partner's debts, decisions or irresponsibilities.

Limited company

By registering as a limited company, the individual or partnership is more protected against liability for damages or losses. However, you do have to register your accounts at Company House, and follow a more stringent set of corporate laws, especially as you will likely become an employee of the company. Also, you have to have at least two directors of a limited company.

The pros and cons of being freelance

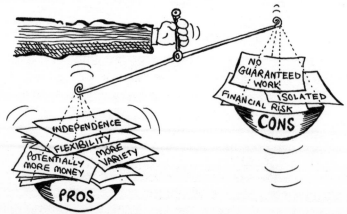

Pros

- Independence
- Flexibility, with own working hours
- Don't necessarily have to commute – reduced expenses and increased time (depending on business)
- Potential for making more money
- Escape office politics
- More variety of work
- Quality of life

Cons

- No guaranteed work or income
- More isolated – reduced human contact
- Financial risk and liability

Why do I want to go freelance?

There are usually two reasons why people go freelance. First, they become unemployed. Second, they choose to leave work to do it. Whichever is the case for you, it is important to understand your own motives and suitability, as this could save an awful lot of time, money and heartache later.

Reasons for going freelance
Tick the ones that are relevant to you

☐ Unemployed
☐ My own decision
☐ It has been an ambition of mine
☐ I want to earn more money*

☐ I want to be the master of my own destiny*
☐ I hate my job*
☐ I hate my boss/company*
☐ I want to change my lifestyle and have more time
☐ I need a challenge*

If you have ticked any with an asterix(*), then think carefully about your reasons. These could be addressed by getting another job and not necessarily by going freelance. Whilst they may figure in the desire to be independent, they are not good enough reasons in themselves for taking the freelance route.

Have I got what it takes?

The life of a freelancer can be extremely lonely. Initially, at least, most freelancers choose to work from home as this helps to cut down on overheads. Depending on the type of service that you can offer, there may be opportunities to work from clients' offices during the stages of various projects. This will help to reduce the isolation.

Characteristics of being a freelancer
Tick those applicable to you

☐ I enjoy my own company
☐ I am self-motivated
☐ I am disciplined
☐ I do not require other people's input all the time in order to get the job done
☐ I can take responsibility and make decisions by myself
☐ I can cope if money and/or work is in short supply
☐ I am not afraid to work extremely hard
☐ I am not afraid of long hours
☐ I am not afraid of short deadlines
☐ I can instigate projects
☐ I can keep smiling, even when the chips are down
☐ I get on with people
☐ I am determined to make it work
☐ I enjoy, and can cope with, change

Whilst the list of characteristics may look a bit bleak, it is better to look at the situation realistically. It is more likely that in real terms you will face a mixture of contradictory situations. You may be extremely busy and then experience a lull. You may be optimistic one day, and then not so cheerful the next. The reality will probably be that your working patterns and approach to work and customers will change radically, and you will need to be flexible in order to adapt to it.

It may be worth talking through the above characteristics with your partner or a close friend to double-check that what you consider to be correct is true. This is especially helpful within a domestic environment. Working from home may highlight a set of difficulties which is worth considering. It is definitely worth making sure that all the people who will be affected by it understand the reasons and implications of your working from home.

Tomorrow we will look at what you need to set yourself up, especially within the home environment. Now, however, you should analyse the effect it could have on you and your loved ones.

Working from home
Discuss the following questions with your partner

- If I have a deadline to meet and have to work long hours, how will we cope?
- Will I be distracted by things around the home, e.g. the TV?
- If I am the only breadwinner, how will this affect us?

- If I have no work, what will be the effect?
- What happens if I'm not earning enough money?
- What happens if we can't take a holiday due to too much work or lack of money?
- How will our social life be affected?
- How are the responsibilities around the home divided to accommodate the change in working patterns?
- Will you be able to cope with my being around the home all the time?

List all your answers, highlighting any potential problems that you can anticipate. Come up with a list of alternatives and solutions to these potential problems.

Now that we've covered the areas of personal analysis and preparation, we will turn to what you are going to offer as a freelancer. Who do you know who will pay you to do it?

What can I offer?

Answering this question means deciding what business you are in, what services you can offer and to whom. Naturally, this will stem from your current work and experience. One of the best pieces of advice I had was to start with something you know about, not something that you like the sound of. Just because you've eaten in a restaurant doesn't mean that you are equipped to open and run a restaurant. To try something completely different is not impossible, but makes the whole process of going freelance harder. It also requires more research.

The questions you need answers to!

- What are my skills?
- What is my experience?
- What do I enjoy doing?
- How can these be adapted to become *services*?
- How do I describe myself, i.e. consultant, researcher?
- What industry/market will I be working in?
- How can my services be targeted towards my chosen industry?
- Is there anyone else doing similar work in my industry? If so, how successful are they?
- Who are my contacts?
- Will they pay for my services?
- Will they pay enough?
- What is the 'going rate'?
- Will there be enough ongoing work?

You need to work hard at answering these questions. Draw up lists for each of them and give honest answers. You could even write a prototype brochure or advert about yourself in order to focus your thinking. Imagine what types of questions potential clients could ask you and what answers you would give. Remember you are going to need to know the ins and outs of your business in some detail if you are to impress prospective clients. Think now why anyone would employ *you* rather than an already existing supplier. If it feels strange to call yourself something like a 'consultant', practice it in front of a mirror until you can say it with a straight face.

At the end of this process you must be able to say 'Yes' to the ultimate question: 'Would I employ myself to do this job?' If the answer is 'No', then you need to rethink your approach until you come up with a confident and honest 'Yes'.

So far we have spent a lot of time looking at personal assessment and analysis. This is important because the psychological and emotional preparation required will help you to focus on your business and work at a later date. It may also help you to avoid making a whimsical decision that could prove disastrous for you, your career and your home life.

Taking the plunge into freelance work is the hardest part. You have to give up the security of work and wages. In turn, this means that you will inevitably feel insecure and vulnerable at the beginning, however much work you have. You won't know whether or not it will carry on being busy. You will find it difficult to say no, and will end up working long hours to get the work done.

Given all these variables, the better prepared you are psychologically and emotionally, the easier it will be to face the variety of different situations that may arise.

Am I ready for it?

Having prepared for the day when you can comfortably say 'I am self-employed', you now need to go on and plan for that day. You need to know what equipment you require, what resources you have, what work you can get immediately and how you can get ongoing work. The preparation is over, and the planning should now begin.

Summary

Today we have looked at:

- What being a freelancer involves
- The pros and cons of being self-employed
- Your motives for wanting to be self-employed
- Whether you are the right type of person to be self-employed
- How the change in circumstances will affect your personal life
- What skills and experience you have
- What business you are in and who your contacts are

Before moving onto the next chapter, look back over your notes, think about all the thoughts and discussions you have had, and stand in front of the mirror, or your family, and say out loud, 'I am ready to become self-employed.' How does it feel?

The first steps

Today we will be looking at what the next stage is after deciding to go freelance. At the end of yesterday you were psychologically and emotionally ready to take the plunge. The next big question is *when* to take the plunge. If you have been made redundant or are unemployed, this decision may have largely been taken for you. If you are choosing to leave work, then you have the luxury of more money, and more time in which to plan for the great day.

FREELANCEDOM

There are certain things that you will need to have at your disposal when you go freelance. Of course, the more time and money you can dedicate to planning for the set-up, the easier it will be. There is nothing worse than turning a job down or getting halfway through a project and thinking, 'I really need this equipment, but I can't afford it!' It would be unrealistic to expect yourself to acquire everything beforehand, but there are some basic, minimum requirements.

Having looked at what you will probably need, we will then go on to plan for setting yourself up with enough work to make a start. But first, what are you actually going to do?

I am a...!

What are you? What are you going to do? What is your business going to be? We looked at this in some depth yesterday, so you should know the answers. However, to know what business you are in will help you to plan the requirements for fulfilling your business expectations. Also, to define in broad terms what your business is going to be will help you in the *future*, as you will have a flexible and open-minded attitude to the different types of work that may come your way.

My business is...!

To help you define your business, here are a couple of examples. A railway company is not in the business of running a railway system. Rather, it is in the business of moving people and goods from A to B. They could do this with buses and cars, but then they would lose the advantage of train travel. The same transport of people and goods is true of British Airways. If, and when, they invent the Star Trek transporter beam, who has the natural claim to use the technology, the railway company or BA? The answer is *either*: whoever invests in it first gets the competitive advantage, and they will still be in the business of transporting people from A to B.

As for myself, I work a lot in the publishing industry, but my definition of publishing is *the transferral of information from source to 'reader', in any format or medium*. Therefore, as a publishing consultant, I don't have to limit myself to just book or magazine publishers.

These examples show the value of thinking clearly and laterally about the business that you are in. Having defined your business, you should now have a clearer idea of what equipment you will need.

Equipment

There are two aspects of business which require some form of equipment. It doesn't matter whether the business is producing or selling something or is purely service based, it will need to be able to communicate with its clients and have the equipment to produce its product. Even in a service industry, such as if you are a researcher, you will need to produce tangible forms of communication. So what do you need?

Telephone/fax
You will almost certainly need a telephone, but do you need a separate business-specific line, or are you willing to use your domestic line and number? If the latter, you may need to investigate obtaining 'cost centre' codes from the telephone company, so that you can differentiate the domestic from business calls on your bill.

What about a mobile phone? It may be good for your image, but is it worth the extra expense? Is it that important that you can constantly be in touch with anybody and everybody? Sometimes it is nice to be uncontactable, although if you are out and about a lot, it makes sense to be at the other end of a phone. Pragmatically speaking, though, you should only really have a mobile phone if it will help you make money.

The other piece of telecommunications equipment is a fax.
Do you see yourself needing to send lots of paper quickly
to your clients when the postal service will do? Saying that,
do you actually live near a post office, so that you can post
your mail quickly and get more stamps when needed? A
fax is undeniably useful, especially as it can be used to
copy important documents, but is it vital? If you do decide
to get a fax machine, you also need to decide whether to go
to the extra expense of having a dedicated fax line installed.
If not, then make sure that you get a model that switches
automatically between incoming phone and fax calls.

It's probably also advisable to get an answering machine,
as you will no longer have colleagues around to take
messages and leave notes. In this case, make sure that your
phone, fax and answering machine are all compatible and
work smoothly together.

Computer
The decision about whether or not to have a computer is a
problematical one. Computers are ubiquitous in the world
today, and yet they also prompt the most fear in people.
Personally, I couldn't imagine working without a computer.
Even if your chosen business is not related to using a
computer, e.g. you are going to be a painter and decorator,
they are indispensable for writing to clients, doing invoices
and keeping accounts and clients' address details. They
also offer the chance to expand as your business expands.
Even if you are willing to do everything on your trusty
typewriter, what happens if you eventually need to employ
a secretary and he or she can only work on a computer?

Choosing a computer requires a great deal of thought, research and hard work, especially as it is likely to be one of the most expensive pieces of equipment you will buy. The computer industry is full of jargon and abbreviations and numbers, but these *do* all mean something and you would be advised to take the time to learn about them. This will make your buying decision easier and help you avoid the hard sell, as many shop assistants themselves don't really know what it all means.

The essential jargon

- Microprocessor (chip) speed, measured in MHz – the higher the number, the faster the machine the less time spent waiting for the machine to do whatever it has to do
- RAM (random access memory) – this is the memory that runs the software. The more memory, the quicker the software runs
- ROM (read only memory)/hard disk – this is the memory that stores all your work. The more you have the more you can store, and you won't need to upgrade as quickly

Software
Buying a computer is only the beginning of the saga. Next you will need to decide on the best software for your needs. Many computers come with software, and it can be expensive to buy separately. The following are the different types of software:

- Word processor – designed for easy writing; ideal for letters, invoices, reports etc
- Database – designed to allow you to manipulate, find and sort information; ideal for names and addresses, i.e. your own mailing list of clients and contacts
- Spreadsheet – designed for numbers and mathematical calculations; ideal for accounting
- Communications software – designed for use with a modem and telephone line; ideal for connection to the Internet, and can be used to send and receive faxes
- Integrated package – a specialist software program that usually incorporates all, or some, of the above

This is a very brief introduction to computers and software.

Finally, if you decide you need to buy a computer, the following points are useful tips:

- Shop around
- Decide what you will use it for
- Get the biggest and fastest machine you can afford
- Check the warranty and technical support (you don't want to lose work due to broken equipment)
- Make back-up copies of your work (you don't want to lose your work and have to start again – ignore this at your peril!)

Stationery and office equipment

There are many things that you take for granted when you work for a company, such as pens and paper, desks, office chairs, filing cabinets, paper clips and rubber bands. Unfortunately, you will have to start paying for these yourself now, but you can at least start to buy your own stocks before you go freelance. You will be amazed at how quickly you will become adept at carefully opening envelopes and Jiffy bags for re-use.

You may wish to consider having stationery and business cards printed. Business cards are a must, but you could set up a letterhead and invoice template on your computer if you wanted to avoid printing costly stationery.

Other equipment

Your equipment requirements will obviously depend on your own line of business. If you are planning to do a sandwich delivery round, you will legally need to refrigerate the food, which has implications for the type of equipment you need. If you are going to be a decorator, then that new ladder may be a must. Whatever it is, think about what you need to buy and how much it will cost. If possible, try to get it before you start. If not, plan for when you *do* need it.

Ultimately, the best thing to do is to acquire only the things that you absolutely need in order to start up. With the bare minimum of equipment, you can earn the money to buy the rest; without it, you can't. However, if you have more than the bare minimum, then you will be making less demands on your cash flow, and at the beginning, you will feel less vulnerable and anxious about your business.

Equipment checklist

Item	Already have	Need now	Need later	Cost
Phone				
Fax				
Answering machine				
Computer				
Printer				
Software				
Printed stationery				
Office supplies				
Desk				
Filing cabinets				
Other items specific to my business				
. . . .				
. . . .				
. . . .				
. . . .				
. . . .				
. . . .				

Where am I going to work?

Where you will physically work is of paramount importance. There are various options, all of which have cost implications. These are: home, separate premises or client's premises. Where you work will be dependent on the type of work you do and the type of space you need for equipment and storage. It may also depend on the type of domestic situation you have.

Home
Working from home is certainly the cheapest option. You dramatically reduce your set-up costs and overheads, and will be eligible for certain tax advantages. It is also the place where you will get the most potential benefits, and possible tensions, from being freelance.

The advantage of home is that you can get out of bed and within 10 seconds be up and ready to start work. You may not have to dress up (or even dress!), you can have music on and the kitchen is handy for refreshments. You don't have to waste time commuting or paying for transport to work. If you do fancy a break, you can have one within a comfortable environment.

The downside of working from home comes from its being the place in which you and your family live. You may not have enough space to set up a separate working environment or to store equipment; you may have children or pets that interrupt and annoy you; and there are domestic distractions: your partner may want you to do the washing up and cleaning – after all, you're at home all day!

It's possible to let yourself go as well. The biscuit tin is within easy reach, you don't need to go out, you may not keep your appearance up as well as you would normally, or the garden/TV may be more interesting than sitting at a desk. You'd be surprised at the number of 'office miles' you walk in a company, so you may need to consider some sort of regular exercise. Another aspect to consider is whether you really want to have your home address and telephone number either on stationery or as 'public property'. (If not, then investigate getting a PO box number and separate phone line.)

Ultimately, it all boils down to the type of person you are, and whether you have the self-discipline not to be distracted and to get on with work. It's not as hard as it sounds, as clients, deadlines, future work and paying the bills provide enough motivation to get down to it.

However, if you feel that you require the discipline of 'going out to work', or that your domestic situation doesn't really lend itself to working from home, then there are other options.

Separate premises

This has many advantages over your home. The first one is that you can choose the type of premises that suits your business. You may be able to have more space and create a more open environment to which you would be happy bringing clients. It may also suit you better psychologically to have a place to go to in order to work. Your own premises will create a structure by which you can separate your work from your personal life. You may also have the opportunity for future expansion.

The disadvantages are that it may actually become a second home, and that you never see the first one. The other issues come down to costs. You will be responsible for funding separate premises, and you will need to be able to cover *all* the expenses. These will include: all utilities, business council tax, separate building and contents insurance, rent/lease, extra phone leads at business rates and travel costs to and from home. You will also have to make sure that it satisfies health and safety regulations, and that you have Public Liability Insurance for all the people who come onto the premises. It is probable that you will need to buy more equipment and furniture to make it fully functional, and you'll end up worrying about the security of it all.

Hot-desking, virtual offices or *tele-cottages* are becoming more popular and common, and are worth researching. The idea behind this is that you either rent space in an office environment, as and when you need it, or use the facilities on offer when you require them. This is great if the type of work you can do is not dependent upon large amounts of equipment and you can carry it around in a briefcase.

Clients' premises

Using clients' premises may offer the best of both worlds, if your business allows you to do this. If you are offering a service that is best fulfilled by working 'in-house', then you will probably need a small base in your home from which to run the business and do the paperwork. As it will only be a base, it is unlikely that you need a separate space that is off limits to the rest of the household. Remember that if you do work on clients' premises, you will have to cover your own travel costs, and more importantly, you will be unable to use just one client's premises, otherwise the Inland Revenue will start to ask you some awkward questions.

Summary

Today we have looked at:

- The type of business you are, and what services you can offer
- The things that you need in order to set yourself up
- Essential equipment and costs
- Where you will work

You need to begin to list all the things that you will want to acquire. This should be structured in terms of *immediate* and *short term*. Research the costs and begin to build up a picture of what your expenditure will be. Tomorrow and the day after, we will be considering the financial aspects of going freelance. Start thinking about how much you need to earn, and what you can charge for your services.

The financial side

Now we must turn our attention to the most interesting, and yet daunting, aspect of going freelance: money. Whether you want to go freelance to make your fortune or just to have a more relaxed way of life, you have to be aware of the financial implications. Today we will look at the formalities of being a freelance. When you work for somebody else they take care of your tax and National Insurance, and maybe such areas as a pension. As a freelancer, however, it is up to you, but you don't need to be a mathematician.

We will be looking at:

- Banks and bank accounts
- Accounts and accountants
- Tax and the Inland Revenue

- National Insurance
- VAT
- Insurances and pensions

The most important thing to remember is that you should not worry: the task is not as intimidating as it seems.

Financial implications of being freelance

What you earn is not all yours and a goodly portion must go to the taxman. With the rest, you should also think about planning for your financial future and developing your business. This expenditure must come on top of whatever you have to spend on keeping your business going in terms of equipment and materials. Only then will you have some money left over to pay yourself, your mortgage and other bills.

Banks and Bank Accounts
You will certainly need to deal with a bank when you go freelance. Your type of business, your savings and the start-up capital you require will determine what type of dealings you have.

The simplest form is as an individual. You open a separate current account in your name and then deposit your earnings into it. If you do not need to borrow from a bank, then this is very straightforward. It also means that you get the advantages of being an individual customer, such as free banking charges. However, if your circumstances change and you need to borrow money or use a company name, then you may have some explaining to do.

If you trade as a business, then you may incur charges, and, therefore, it will be worth shopping around to negotiate the best deals.

If you need to borrow money, then you will be required to do a business plan in order to convince the bank manager that you are worth investing in. (We will look at business plans on Saturday.) All the banks have managers who specialise in small businesses, and they will all want your business plan presented in a certain way. They are very helpful and produce a lot of bumph to help you, so it is best to do some research first.

When looking for the best deals, you should also think about various types of accounts. For instance, it may be worth having a higher-interest account for paying direct debit bills (such as pensions, NI, etc). It will also be worth having a separate, high-interest account for putting your tax money away.

It is vital for you to find yourself a good bank that you are happy doing business with. Not only is a good bank/bank manager worth their weight in gold, but it is imperative that you have a separate work account, away from your domestic one. This will make your accounting considerably easier.

Accounts and accountants
You will need to keep track of all your revenues and expenses; and you will need to keep a set of accounts. In simple terms, your accounts will list all your revenues on one side and all your expenses on the other. If your expenses are tax deductible, then you will only be taxed on what excess 'profit' is remaining. Essentially, it is an 'in and out' system.

Some suggested headings for a simple accounting system

Income
Date, Job, Client, Invoice number, Amount, VAT, Total

Expenditure
Date, Item, Equipment, Stationery/postage, Subsistence/travel, Marketing, Petty cash, Amount, VAT, Total

Headings such as these will normally go across the top of your accounts book horizontally, and will work as headings for each column.

For example:

INCOME

Date	Job	Client	Invoice Number	Amount	VAT	Total

You will vary the types of column depending on the different aspects to your business, but this does give some idea of what is required. You may find it helps to also have columns for a code which is cross-referenced to your receipts, and also a column to describe the type of payment method, e.g. cheque, debit, cash. The VAT is there in case you think there will be some benefit in being VAT registered (see below).

The Inland Revenue has simplified its systems to make returns easier. One of the steps is to introduce a lower ceiling, so if your turnover (the sum of all revenues or 'ins') is under the ceiling, all you have to do is to submit a three-line statement, indicating:

- Turnover
- Expenses
- Profit

For up-to-date information on what that ceiling figure is, contact your nearest HM Inspector of Taxes office.

If you earn over that limit, then you need to submit a proper set of accounts which detail your revenue and expenses. These should be supported by copies of invoices and receipts. It is worth keeping all invoices and receipts even if you do not earn the minimum amount required for the lower ceiling, as the Inland Revenue could ask you to justify your accounts if they so desire. Accounts can also be done on a computer and there are now many software packages available to help with this and Self Assessment (see below).

Setting up and doing your accounts yourself will save you money, as you will not have to pay an accountant. You can also submit your accounts to the Inland Revenue yourself, without the services of an accountant, but it is probably better to use an accountant, if only for your tax returns.

It is advisable, in the beginning, to do your own accounts and then have your accountant check them before submission. The advantage, apart from saving money, is that you will know what state your business is in. Although your tax returns are done annually, only an ongoing knowledge of your financial situation means that you will know whether you are being paid on time and who you should chase for payment. Try to get into the habit of keeping your accounts up to date. Entering your expenses after you come home in the evening is so much quicker and easier than trying to remember what a receipt was for 12 months down the line. It will also mean that your accountant will spend less time sorting through your accounts, and this will save you money.

Having an accountant will make your life easier. A good accountant with a good reputation is invaluable. The Inland Revenue has so much work to go through that it cannot chase and cover every submission. Therefore, they will take a lot of the returns on trust; if they trust an accountant, they are more likely to accept their returns, and you will experience less hassle and get your tax returns accepted more quickly.

Once again, shop around for a good accountant or accountancy firm. Most accountants will arrange a 'consultancy session' free of charge. Prepare your list of what you need to know, don't be afraid to ask what you consider to be dumb questions, help them to help you set up a good accounting system. They make their money on fees, which could increase with the amount of time spent doing your accounts, so it is in your interest to set up a good system that works quickly and smoothly. Ask what they will charge you.

Tax deductible items

- Equipment (capital allowances which are equivalent to a depreciation allowance)
- Materials
- Travel expenses, including use of private car for business only, and petrol if definitely for business purposes only
- Subsistence – food and hotels (if definitely for business purposes)
- Office premises, or a percentage for working from home
- Insurances
- Utility bills (gas, electricity, phone), or a percentage for working from home
- Accountant's fees
- Pensions (tax deductible, although they are not usually put into your accounts)

Tax and the Inland Revenue

This is the dreaded bit: tax. You have to pay tax, but first you have to inform your local HM Inspector of Taxes about your change in status from employed/unemployed to self-employed. You will need to send them a copy of your last P45 and also state the date on which you started trading. This date will be the beginning of your financial year, unless you rearrange it. You can only rearrange it from the date of the end of your trading period.

You will pay tax at the same level as everybody else. There are various tax brackets which apply to everybody, and which vary from Budget to Budget. The tax you pay will correspond to how much profit you earn, and which bracket that falls into. Check with the Inland Revenue and/or your accountant for the latest brackets. You will still be eligible for your normal tax allowances, such as single/married-persons allowance.

Tax is collected twice a year, in January and July. However, as yours is a new business the Inland Revenue doesn't have a record of what you have earned, and therefore has no history on which to base its claim. As a result, you will probably not have your first assessment and tax return until at least 12 months into the business. This doesn't mean that you won't pay any tax on what you earn in this period: you will. It *does* mean that the taxman may not ask for it until 12 months or so in the future. Personally, I cannot recommend strongly enough the need for you to put aside money for the day when you have to pay the Inland Revenue. I would recommend that you put 30% of everything you earn into a building society account and leave it there. If you go over the higher tax bracket, do not forget to increase your savings. You should only touch it when you need to pay your tax bill. To not pay tax is a criminal offence, although it is up to your accountant to advise you on how to reduce your tax bill.

I would urge you not to try to beat the taxman; at the end of the day, you will be losing enough sleep worrying about the business and work without waiting for the taxman to come knocking on your door.

Self Assessment

Self Assessment is a new method of submitting tax returns. This is not a new tax, rather a simplification of existing methods of assessing and paying tax.

Up until Self Assessment, the Inland Revenue was responsible for deciding how much tax you had to pay, based on your accounts and tax return. Under Self Assessment, *you* will now be responsible for that decision. Self Assessment combines your tax return and assessment for all your sources of income, your reliefs, deductions and allowances, all for one year. You will be expected to enter all the figures onto the Tax Return form, without referring back to your accounts books. You do need to keep accounts, though, in case any reference does need to be made to them later by you, your accountant or the Inland Revenue. There are also explicit dates for returns and payments. Failure to comply will result in penalty payments and interest being charged.

The Inland Revenue has produced a range of information booklets which explain the system in detail. Contact your local Inland Revenue office for them.

National Insurance (NI)
The Department of Social Security will keep a record of whether or not you pay your 'stamps'. Non-payment could affect your state pension and other social security benefits. In the light of this, don't ignore it.

When you work for somebody else, you pay a percentage of your salary on NI Class 1 contributions. When you become self-employed you change to Class 2 contributions, whereby you pay a flat weekly fee to the DSS. You will also pay a percentage of your profits, which are called Class 4 contributions.

You must register with the DSS to say that you are self-employed. Do not assume that the Inland Revenue will do it, because they won't. Contact your nearest Department of Social Security for details about NI contributions and what the weekly cost is. They will provide you with plenty of information about it, plus a direct debit form.

VAT

VAT (Value Added Tax) is not complicated, but you do need to have serious discussions about it with your accountant and with HM Customs and Excise who are responsible for administering it. The latter will help with free introductory videos and one-to-one consultations; find them in your telephone directory.

Everybody pays VAT on goods and services where applicable, and the advantage of being VAT registered is that you can claim the VAT back on business expenses – again where applicable. You do not need to be VAT registered unless your annual turnover exceeds a certain figure, when it becomes compulsory. Your accountant can advise you of the most recent and relevant figure. You can volunteer to be VAT registered, though. This is advantageous if you know that your turnover will exceed the ordained limit, or if you are buying a lot of equipment or services.

It may also be worth registering if you are handling goods or services for your client. For instance, if you buy VAT items which you are then invoicing your customer for but you are not VAT registered, you will probably put the cost of the VAT on your invoice. If, in addition, they *are* registered, they will not be able to claim it back. If you are registered and they can claim VAT back, you will be more competitively priced.

One tip about VAT: if you have an inkling that you may need or want to be registered, include a VAT column in your accounts as this will save time and work later. It will also help you to compile and submit your first VAT returns. (See Accounts and Accountants section above.)

Insurances and pensions
There are various aspects of insurance that you need to be aware of. First, does your domestic house insurance cover you for office equipment and working from home? Second, does your car insurance cover business use? Obviously, if you have separate business premises or vehicles you will need to have separate insurance policies, but if not you should check it out.

Don't assume that existing policies will cover you, don't hope that it will never happen to you, and don't trust in your ability to fool your insurance company if anything does happen. Be prepared to pay a little more on your premiums.

You should also consider professional indemnity insurance, especially if you are not a limited liability company. This will cover you for any damages claims made against you due to negligence. If you are not covered, your personal and private assets may be at risk.

What happens if you can't work because of illness or disability? If so, you will be without any income, and then who knows what will happen. To cover this, investigate some form of income protection policy.

Also, have a good look at pensions. It is worth preparing for the future, although it can be difficult to find the premiums to start with. If you have any 'profit' left over at the end of your financial year, you can deposit up to a certain percentage of your annual profit into a pension scheme and it will be tax deductible. The percentage will vary according to your age: the older you are, the higher the percentage. Investigate a pension that will allow you both to pay a monthly premium and also contribute a lump sum. If you have had a company pension scheme in the past, investigate the possibility of transferral, but don't do it unless it is advantageous.

In all these cases, find yourself a good independent financial advisor (IFA), who must be registered with the Personal Investment Authority (PIA). Shop around again, and choose the one that you feel you can trust. Let them know that you are shopping around, and don't forget to ask what their commission is; they have to tell you by law. Having a good IFA will complement your accountant, although many accountancy firms will have trained IFAs in-house. Your accountant will make sure that your business is healthy, and an IFA will help you make sure that your personal financial situation is healthy.

In the same way as you may have a bank account for your tax money, it may be worth having a separate account for paying the monthly premiums on insurance, pensions and the like. There are various types of account which pay a better rate of interest, but allow for direct debit transactions to occur. Investigate and you could make some extra interest, while securing some peace of mind.

Summary

Today we have looked at those financial aspects of going freelance that you will have to face. Unfortunately, these are the logistics of running a business. They are not directly related to the work that you want to do, but they have to be done. In saying that, it should also be stressed that if you establish your systems at the outset and are disciplined in keeping on top of them, then they should present you with very little work and few, if any, problems.

It is important to remember that tax allowances and levels of contributions change regularly, usually with each Budget. Make sure you ask your accountant to provide you with new information as it changes.

Having dealt with the 'grown-up' and responsible financial side of running a business, we will turn our attention tomorrow to the more fun side of business: making money and a profit.

~~y

To.   .il be turning our attention to the actual
mone,   .king aspect of going freelance. After all, the
chance to earn money for yourself is presumably one of the
reasons you are thinking about being freelance. We will be
looking at:

- Attitude to money
- Cash flow
- What you've been earning and what you need to
  earn to survive
- Setting the right price
- Keeping control of your costs and assessing
  whether you are actually making money
- Projected income
- Credit control
- Tips and hints for making life easier

Attitude to money

Earning your own money is incredibly satisfying, although
it would be naive to say that you will become fabulously
wealthy, especially overnight. However, you will be able to
look at your accounts or bank balance and say to yourself,
'I made that'; and you may feel for the first time in your
career that you have earned the right money for the right
job, without making unknown shareholders richer. Even if
you are making less money than before, you will, hopefully,
feel the direct correlation between what you do and the
amount you earn.

The motives for going freelance are multifarious and complex, and money is only one aspect. It would be dangerous to focus solely on the financial rewards, as you might become too concerned about screwing the last penny out of your customers. Initially, you will not have a strong enough and loyal enough client base for you to be too rigid in your money dealings with them; you will need a certain flexibility in the way that you work and deal with clients, and if you come across as too unbending, you will lose them. On the other hand, be aware that customers may not pay you, and the level of flexibility that you give them will reflect this. A good client is one that gives you work *and* pays you.

Being flexible, willing and helpful is going to buy you goodwill, which you will start to cash in on later. Building good working relationships from the start will mean repeat business, and repeat business means more work and more income. The financial costs of constantly getting new customers to replace the ones you've lost is considerably higher than that of keeping existing ones happy.

Having said all this and painted a happy-go-lucky picture of a carefree life with fast-flowing cash and no worries, you do need to build money into your equation. After all, the purpose of a business is to give value to the owner, and one of the best ways of giving value is to make money. If you don't make any money, or enough money, you'll find that being freelance isn't such a good idea, and you'll soon be brushing up your curriculum vitae and applying for jobs.

Cash flow

You need a smart attitude to money and the way that it underpins your business and, in turn, your life.

One aspect of being smart is adapting to the change in circumstances. If you've been working and receiving a regular income, then you expect to receive some money at the end of every week or month. You can order your expenditures around pay-day; however deeply in the red you are, you know that for a brief moment every month, the pain will be eased slightly.

The change that you have to prepare for involves not just the irregularity of the work, but also of the payments. At the start-up, you will experience a greater time lag. You will spend time doing the work and then waiting for the money. It is likely, and usual, for your customers to expect a period of credit. This time lag can be extremely unsettling and you need to be prepared.

The light at the end of the tunnel is that when you are paid, especially if it is a sizeable amount, you suddenly have more money than you would have normally. Not only are you solvent, but you need to make some decisions about what you do with it. Here are some clues:

- Put 30% aside for Tax
- Buy some equipment you need
- Pay yourself
- Save it

The last is the most prudent as your cash flow will be subject to the time lags inherent in doing and billing work. You may have money now, but what about next month, or the month after? Avoid the temptation to fritter it away, as so often happens with salaries. If you can get into the habit of being careful and only covering the expenses that you have to, then you will be able to ride the periods when you don't have any work. If you are lucky enough to have more than enough work all through the year, then think of all the money you have saved!

If you are fortunate to have a lot of money left towards the end of your financial year, book an appointment with your accountant and seek advice on the best way of using the money profitably, and for tax deductions.

Remember, poor cash flow is the most common cause of new business failure, even those with full order books!

What you've been earning and what you need to survive

Up to now you have probably been used to a regular income, which you have spent according to your outgoings. Those outgoings are likely to have been purely personal and domestic. As we have seen already, a smart attitude to your money and your cash flow is required. Couple your domestic needs with your business and start-up costs, and then you will begin to build a picture of the type of income you need to be generating in order for your freelance business to be worth your while.

On Monday, we saw that the start-up costs and cost of equipment can be considerable, on top of your personal requirements. The best thing to do is to break each part down into its constituent parts. The numbers will vary depending on your situation, but we'll look at all of them; discount any that are not applicable to your situation.

Domestic budget

Usual outgoings

- Mortgage/rent
- Council Tax
- Insurance policies
- Pensions, etc
- Bills – telephone, gas, electricity, water rates
- Car costs – insurance, tax, petrol, servicing and repairs – how many cars have you got?
- Food
- Clothing
- HP agreements and loans repayments

- Holidays
- Children and other family costs, such as entertainment, toys, personal luxuries
- Overdrafts
- Credit card bills

Usual income

- Before tax
- After tax
- Partner's income before tax?
- Partner's income after tax?

What is your final monthly income as a household? What is the difference between the two? Think ahead 6–12 months into the future. Have you got any expenditure coming up or plans that require money? Have you booked a holiday that will need financing? Are you planning on starting a family or moving house, or is your car likely to 'give up the ghost'?

You need to make sure that you have covered all the angles. Looking back at the thoughts and calculations you made on Monday, what are your start-up costs going to be? Add your existing domestic outgoings to your proposed start-up costs. What does the figure look like? Do you have enough savings or enough proposed work to pay the bills for the first couple of months? If not, will you have to get financing from your bank? If so, is your proposal good enough to warrant the capital?

You now have enough raw data to help you begin to set the right price. This will also go a long way to help you with a business plan if you do need the financial help of your bank.

Setting the right price

There are two factors in trying to set the right price: what the market will pay and what you need to earn.

Unfortunately, the market rate is by far the most important. Nobody is going to pay over the odds just because you need more money to pay your bills; you're running a business, not a charity.

Working from the assumption that you are going freelance in an area of business that you have had first-hand experience of, you should have a pretty good idea of what the going market rates are. If you don't, then you've got some more research to do to find out what these are. One good thing to bear in mind, though, is that you can be flexible with your pricing. Using a market rate is a good springboard, but ultimately you charge what your customer is willing to pay. If one customer pays more for the same job than another customer, then so be it. The essence is to make sure that your customer doesn't feel cheated or that they have paid over the odds. One way of doing this is to 'add value', which we will cover later on in the week.

The second factor in setting the price is what you need to earn. Your calculations from the above sections will help you in determining this. However, there is an important mental lesson to learn. If you are quoting, and billing, large sums of money for work, you are likely to feel apprehensive as you will not be used to so much money. By the same token, don't *underprice*: if your price is too low, people will question the quality.

Our sense of our own worth is conditioned by the salaries that we have been paid. If you propose to do a job in two weeks and you get paid more than you would for a month's salary, it is understandable that you will feel apprehensive. Be confident in your pricing, but not greedy. It is vital to remember that you may not be earning anything two months down the line and you will still have bills to pay.

Now we should look at how to confidently price your products or services. The price of your product will be directly comparable to that of a competing product in the market-place. The customer may choose on quality, and if you want to charge a premium price, you have to be able to demonstrate that your product is of better quality. The price will also be affected by the cost of production, in terms of both materials and time.

With products, when comparing price and what you need to earn, you also have to build in a quantity factor. If you can sell the product at the right price but do not sell enough, then you won't realise your expectations. This moves us into marketing and distribution issues, which you should be aware of. If you are not, you should do more research, or rethink your ideas.

Services are easier to price because you are selling time and expertise, which is similar to being employed to bring your expertise to a company for a period of time each day. Therefore, you can calculate how much you were paid by the hour by your employer. This could become a minimum for you to work from. Alternatively, you could divide your requirements for each month by the number of hours you wish to work in a month, to get a per-hour rate.

At this point you are trying to establish the minimum requirements that you wish to achieve. In the long term, the aim is to earn more, as this will help you through the lulls and/or allow you to expand or just have more money at your disposal.

The major concern for every freelancer should be to cover costs; that will be the primary aim for each financial year. Levels of profit and profitability will differ from person to person and will match their ambitions and desires, but everybody needs to cover their minimum costs.

Keeping control of your costs and assessing whether you are actually making money

Your minimum costs are also fluid, as there will be expense incurred in the actual fulfilment of a job. This might be as simple as the cost of paper, envelopes, stamps and telephone calls, but they still have to be paid for. You can either take a flexible approach and just pay for them as required, or you can monitor your costs and assign them to particular projects or jobs. You can even do this with time, and monitor how much time you have spent on a project or with a customer. By treating time as an asset, you are beginning to improve your sense of the business.

The benefits of monitoring time and costs are various. You will be able to control your costs, so that you remain profitable; you will be able to set better and more accurate prices in the future; and you will be able to make business decisions about what work to accept or not, and in which direction you wish to take your business.

If this sounds too bureaucratic for you, don't worry: it doesn't have to be done. But you do need to think about some ways of monitoring your income versus expenditure on an ongoing basis in order to avoid waking up one morning to discover that your business is costing you more than it makes you. The ramifications of this are many, and contain various degrees of disaster.

Examples of simple cost and time sheets

Time sheet   Job title _____   Client _____

Date	Action	Start	Finish	Amount of time

Amount earned

No. of hours

Cost per hour _____

Cost sheet   Job title _____   Client _____

Date	Item	Quantity	Cost

Amount earned _____

Total cost _____

Keep a record of what you have used to complete a job, how long it has taken you and how much you have earned. From this you can work out how profitable the job has been. It will also help you to price similar jobs in the future.

Projected income

Everybody knows the saying, 'Speculate to accumulate'. It implies risk, and all business – and especially going freelance – is a risk. The task of business is not just to accept the risk but to minimise it, so that your speculation is more likely to result in accumulation.

The purpose of looking at the financial side to working freelance is to plan for minimising the risk factor, and it is not enough to know what you need to achieve. You need to know whether you *can* achieve it or not. You will need to project your income, based on what you know, who you know and where it is possible to get work. You will have a good feeling about doing this just before you go freelance, as you will be laying the foundations before you finally take the plunge.

Even so, you should estimate how much work and income you will be able to achieve. This is especially important if you are trying to raise finance, or have to commit to definite production runs. The objective is to make sure that your income figures exceed your outgoings. This is extremely easy if you lie and over-inflate your expectations, but you should avoid such deceptions, especially as you will have to justify your figures by your actual performance. The key is to be realistic. One way is to put down the best figures you can realistically expect and then halve them. Do they still look good? If so, halve them again. Find the break-even point, as you will then see what actual work and effort you have to put in to break even. Is it possible, and over what time-scale? You need to be able to achieve break even as quickly as possible.

If your business and personal circumstances mean that you don't need to worry about it too much, then don't. I *would* say, however: think about it carefully and get some understanding of what you are trying to achieve. If you don't know where you are going, how will you know if you have got there?

Credit control

One of the most common reasons for businesses going out of business is not lack of work but lack of payment. Effective credit control not only maximises your cash flow but will help you to avoid taking on work from risky credit sources.

Customers will usually require some sort of credit period. It is usually 30 days, but check with your customer, and put your credit terms on your invoice, e.g. 'To be paid within 30 days'. Be prepared to supply new customers with your tax code and any other information in order for them to set up a supplier account for you on their systems. Strangely, they will not request this information when they first receive your invoice but will ask for it when you chase them for payment. Suddenly, 30 days' credit becomes 60 days, or even longer.

At the beginning, you can always try to negotiate an instalment payment to help with your cash flow, or a quicker-than-usual payment of your invoice. You are likely to get it if your first customers are your old company, friends or contacts. They will be more understanding than people who don't know you, but don't come to expect it.

Keeping control of your invoices should not be arduous. In fact, it could be fun, as you get the satisfaction of getting the money in your hands. The following are some tips on how to make it effective:

- As soon as the job is finished, send out the invoice, as the credit period runs from the date of the invoice. It is possible to forget to send an invoice promptly when you are extremely busy
- Always put an invoice number, date, correct company name and address, credit terms, to whom payment should be made, and your VAT Registration Number (if applicable) onto the invoice. Many companies have highly sophisticated and computerised accounting systems which need all the correct information before payment is made. If it isn't on the invoice, valuable credit time is used up supplying it
- Check that the customer has received your invoice and that everything is correct. This is especially important with new customers
- Make sure that you know what invoices are outstanding and when they are due to be paid. Chase them as soon as they are overdue. This sets a precedent for prompt payment with your customers

- When you receive the money, bank it as soon as possible. Apart from cheques taking time to clear, you could be earning interest too

Tips and hints for making life easier

In the build-up to going freelance, there is a great deal that you can do to make the transition from regular income to irregular income easier. Here are just a few ideas to save you time and money whilst contributing to peace of mind for the future.

- Cut down on your expenditure one or two months before going freelance. This will help shield you from some of the shock
- Sort out your financial affairs, such as insurances, etc
- Look at how the bills come in and what the usual amounts are. See if it is possible to stagger them when they come in. For instance, if you have to renew your car insurance and road tax, and put the car through an MOT all in the space of a month or two, you know that this is going to be a major expense. Why not buy a six-month tax disk next time, just to stagger the impact?
- Start to pay bills by direct debit. You will quickly get into the habit of paying them, and will know what your monthly outgoings are more accurately. It also avoids unexpectedly large bills arriving

- Stock up on objects that you think you may not be able to afford, such as shoes and clothes, especially if they are bought in a sale
- Do your Christmas shopping early while you've got the money
- Start to consider what you could do without if necessary

Summary

Today we have looked at the financial aspects of being freelance and the way in which it will affect your business and possibly your lifestyle. We have tried to achieve a balanced overview of what working for yourself entails fiscally. Important factors include:

- Your attitude and motivation about money
- What you need in order to survive, both commercially and personally
- How you price your products/services and keep control of the costs involved
- Cash flow and credit
- Adapting to the change in circumstances

Prudence and diligence in working through the financial aspects will be well worth the effort. You should be more profitable, less stressed by money worries and more able to concentrate on getting work. Good planning minimises risk and reduces nasty shocks.

Maintaining the work flow

So far we have done a great deal of the 'logistical foundation work' needed in order to go freelance. You now have a clearer picture and understanding of what it will take, and, hopefully, you are ready to go for it.

Even if you have the determination, the right personality, the finances and the right business idea to work for yourself, you still need an essential and vital ingredient: the work itself! Plus, you need the skills and qualities to get, do, and keep getting the work.

In this chapter we will be looking at:

- Responsibility – attitude to work
- Reliability and flexibility – the customer is king!
- Decisiveness – learning to say 'No!'
- Sales and negotiating – getting and keeping work
- Marketing – portfolio and word-of-mouth recommendations
- Durability – the highs and lows

Responsibility – attitude to work

That's it, you've decided to go freelance and work for yourself. You are eager and enthusiastic, but you still need to assess what you can do beforehand in order to prepare yourself.

Once you have left your job, you have not only left the security of a regular income, social contact and all the other things we've talked about, but you have also left a comfort zone where you have multiple scapegoats and dogsbodies. Everything you do as a freelancer is up to you.

- If anything goes wrong, it's probably your fault
- If anything doesn't get done, it's probably your fault
- If business is not peforming as well as expected, it's probably your fault

Not only that, but you will be responsible for doing everything yourself. You will have to do your own accounting, your own letters, your own sales and marketing, and, of course, the work itself. You will have no secretary or receptionist (unless/until you can afford to employ one!), and if you are not in the 'office' you will have no colleagues to cover for you.

You will have to prepare yourself to do not only the things you enjoy doing but also the boring bits. Added together, all these different aspects of being freelance may mean that you will have to work extremely long hours in order to get everything done. Fortunately, when you start up, you will probably find that the amount of paperwork and filing will not be as much as you are used to, as you will be the only one generating it.

It is worth setting up your own systems and standards by which you have to work from the outset. Although this sounds rather bureaucratic it will help you to keep on top of everything and save you time and energy. Also, they are *your* systems, designed by you *for* you and not imposed by a larger company structure.

There is one final area concerning your attitude to work. Charles Handy has covered it nicely when he talks about the Type 2 Accountability Error in *The Empty Raincoat*. The essence of this is that there are two types of error that occur in business: first, there is that error where you have done something wrong; and second, there is the missed opportunity.

The missed opportunity is important as it can directly affect the way your business grows and develops. Following up leads, contacts and ideas can lead to more work and business, and it is up to you to do it, especially as you have nobody else to blame if you don't.

Reliability and flexibility - the customer is king!

It is an old adage, but very apt. It encapsulates all the trendy business concepts of marketing, Total Quality Management, customer-focus theory and customer service.

Keeping your customers happy is vital as they can make or break your business. As yours is an independent or small business, every pound they spend with you is significant. Getting new customers is considerably more expensive than satisfying existing customers.

You do not have to be sycophantic with your customers, but you do have to give them the right product/service at the right price, on time. This is difficult when you have many jobs on the go at the same time. You need to be able to juggle your jobs, clients and time to avoid making mistakes, letting somebody down and, ultimately, losing goodwill and your reputation.

I also firmly believe that a healthy, long-term, profitable business is built on good relationships between people. At the end of the day, your customer is a person, not an alien entity. People make decisions not just on price, but also on service, trust, compatibility, honesty and quality of work. All in all, it is about *added value*.

Decisiveness – learning to say 'No!'

As with all relationships, there is a time to say, 'No'. It is especially difficult, however, to say no to work at the beginning. You will be worried that there may not be any more work in the short term, and you will feel that you should accept every job you are offered. You will be anxious that if you say no, your client will never give you any more work in the future.

These are very real worries, and it will be easier to turn work down if you have more than you can physically do. However, you will need to say no if you do have too much or if you really are not competent to do the job properly. It will be better to explain to the customer the reasons for saying no, especially if you can explain it in a way that shows it is beneficial to them, and then you will score many 'brownie' points.

For example, don't say 'I'm too busy at the moment, come back next week'. Instead, say that you are too busy, and that although you could squeeze it in, you feel that they wouldn't get a proper job done – that the extra work could affect the quality of your work both for them and for your other clients. This shows that you care for their business as well; you are adding value to yourself and your business.

Saying no is not just limited to not taking work on: it also has to do with the type of work. The customer may be king, but they are not always right. You should be able to say that, in your expert opinion, they should do something not this way but rather that way. This should be done in a positive and negotiating way, and you should outline all possibilities and scenarios. Remember that you are being employed for your skills, time and expertise. More often than not, your client is solving a problem (i.e. lack of time or in-house experience), so help them to solve the problem cost-effectively. In so doing, you will be able to add value again to your image and reputation, whilst being able to say no.

Sales and negotiating - getting and keeping work

There are two types of people that you can get work from:

- Those that know you
- Those that do not

You will get work not because you are good at what you do but because people *know* that you are good. A proven track record speaks for itself. Potential customers will be more inclined to give you a chance if they like you and you can demonstrate that you are good.

The people that you can most quickly demonstrate these qualities to are those who know you personally. Start your freelance career by approaching:

- Employers
- Friends, especially if they are in your business
- Contacts

A lot of planning and forethought should go into how you can best leave your company and take some work with you. There are two things that you should do to prepare yourself. The first is to decide what you can offer and write a proposal that you can present to them. The second is not to get into awkward situations with your colleagues. It is almost 100% guaranteed that if you stick two fingers up to your bosses and tell them what you think of them, you will not get any work from them. If you do get work from your employers, it demonstrates that the reason you left them was not their dissatisfaction with your work. Having said all of this, even if you are as sweet as pie, there is no guarantee that your employer will give you your first contract.

This is where friends can help. If you have a lot of friends in your chosen field, then you can start to acquire work from them. This also adds to your client base and increases your reputation. Where possible, start to talk to trusted friends about your plans to go freelance and gauge their reaction.

Contacts, depending on how well they know you, are next on the list, as they have some knowledge of you already. They should be contacted once you have gone freelance and have done some work for other people. You should begin to draw up your list of contacts immediately.

Once you have attained some momentum and credibility, then you can move on to breaking new ground.

With regard to all of the above, you need to be able to negotiate in order to actually get the work. There are plenty of training courses and books on negotiating skills, but the essentials you need to remember are:

- Choosing the correct time and place
- Knowing your objectives
- Knowing what you can offer and why you are better than anybody else
- Planning your strategy
- Finding out what your customer wants
- Handling objections
- Talking to the right person, e.g. somebody who can make a decision
- Following up

Having got the work, how do you keep it? Bearing in mind what we have said about the 'customer being king', you must attend to the fact that you are only as good as your last job. If you have done a good job before, then people will come back to you. If you mess a job up, you will have a hard time convincing people to work with you again.

Even when you are not working with people, you should still keep in touch with your client base and contacts. You need to be remembered for when they do need your services. If possible, try to work towards and negotiate a contract of supply or a retainer. You may have to lower the price, but the regularity of income and cash flow is the benefit you require. This will also help you to expand should you wish to.

Marketing – portfolio and word-of-mouth recommendations

Marketing is closely connected with publicity, sales and negotiation. Without getting too deeply into what marketing is, all we need to say is that it is the activity of matching your products/services to the needs and wants of a target market. This is usually achieved using publicity, and, if successful, it results in sales.

Most marketing is associated with high-profile activities such as advertising, catalogues, leaflets, direct mail shots and telephone marketing. Unfortunately, high profile usually means high price. As a freelance, you will not be in a position to employ these methods as you will not have the money or time to do them.

Even so, there *are* ways to market yourself. Marketing involves giving your 'targeted' potential customers information both about yourself and about the benefits of using your products/services. The key to successful marketing is making sure that you match the information you give to the needs of your 'target market'.

For your own activities, you should know your market before you consider going freelance, but there are various things that you can do cheaply in order to market yourself and to prove your track record and credibility.

- Give some business cards to friends and clients to pass around
- Ask clients to recommend you to others within their organisation or industry; only do this if they are pleased with your work. Word-of-mouth recommendations are better than personal 'hype'
- Ask clients if they know of other people that you can contact
- Put your contact details in anything that is being distributed to large numbers of people, where possible. This is useful if you have been involved in a project which is going to be printed
- Go to relevant exhibitions and wander around the exhibitors' stands looking for contacts and clients

> • Prepare a portfolio of work done; include
>   recommendations from satisfied customers

However, marketing is not just about how you present yourself to the market. It is also about what you know about your market and how you take advantage of that knowledge. The more you know about the market, the more you will be able to match your products/services to the market's needs. This in turn will enable you to match your benefits to your market. For example, ask a prospective client what they require before you tell them what you can offer. That way you can match what you can do to their needs. If you do this, you stand a better chance of getting the work.

Durability – the highs and lows

Whatever you do, it is almost certain that you will experience highs and lows in your work. Sometimes you will be so busy you'll wonder why you ever went freelance. At other times you will be in a lull, wondering if you'll ever work again. You will have experienced these lulls when employed, but the effects were reduced because work is created by organisations to fill these lulls.

Think about the lulls you have experienced before. Are they typical for your industry? If they are, can you plan for your lulls and be better prepared for them? If you expect a lull in August, can you plan to go on holiday?

You could also plan to learn something new during a lull. When you work for a company you are paid to learn new things and be trained in some way. In using a lull to learn something new, you can add to your skills and possibly provide new openings for work. You should plan for when you will be working. This, in fact, can be a period of strategic planning.

The important thing to do during a lull is to try not to be depressed. Try not to lose your motivation or discipline. Keep in touch with your clients. And above all, make sure that you have budgeted enough money both to live on and to market your business.

Lulls are not the end of the world, but be prepared for them and use the time productively.

Summary

Today we have looked at how to prepare yourself for getting and keeping work. This has involved:

- Your attitude to work and customers
- People you know who might give you work
- How to market yourself cheaply and effectively
- What to do when you hit a lull

Life matters

Today we will be examining in more detail the effect that going freelance will have on your life. We will be putting all the different aspects of freelancing into a coherent whole. You should then be able to see at a glance the potential impact this could have on you and your own personal situation.

We will be looking at:

- The personal impact – questions and doubts
- The impact on family and friends
- Time management and discipline
- Sickness and back-up
- The future

The personal impact – questions and doubts

Where possible it is good to set a date for when you plan to go freelance. You will also need to give the Inland Revenue a date from which you became self-employed. Once you have made up your mind to go freelance and you have the support of the people around you, start preparing for the Big Day.

You will start to think in terms of going freelance. You'll probably start to:

- Talk to people you meet as if they are potential clients
- Keep notes on people and their requirements
- Compile your database

There is a good chance that you will go through mood swings, being exhilarated one day and worried the next, wondering whether you are doing the right thing. The question 'What if it fails?' will probably flit through your mind, closely followed by 'If it does, will I get another job?' After all, nobody wants to employ a 'failure'.

| EXHILARATED | WORRIED |

Comfort can be found in the fact that all business involves a risk and in becoming freelance you have shown that you have enough courage to take a calculated risk. The main thing is not to worry. If it goes wrong, you either start again or get a job, confident that you have learnt more from doing your own thing than from just being safely tucked away behind a desk. Besides, if you decide that you can't do it, will you get to retirement age thinking 'I wish I had done that'? Will you live with that wish hanging over you? I doubt it.

While preparing for the day when you can say, 'I am my own boss', be careful about the work that you are currently in. It is a bit like anticipating a holiday: the nearer you get the more distracted you become. Watch that you do not become so distracted that you start to underperform in your present work. This will draw attention to yourself, and you may find yourself in a tricky situation. If you think that you have a good chance of getting work from your existing employer, then it is even more important to keep your standards of professionalism and diligence high.

Once you are freelance you will be faced with that vast expanse of time called The Day. How do you fill it? Working for other people is good in that it does provide a structure for at least eight hours of the day. The other good thing about this is that it usually provides the same structure for the vast majority of other working people, such as family and friends.

What you do with your time and how you order your day and do your work throws up some interesting dilemmas that you need to be aware of.

The impact on family and friends

The impact that being freelance can have on family and friends is enormous, both positively and negatively. More importantly, it could affect *you* more, depending on how much emphasis you place on things like time spent relaxing, pursuing hobbies or having a social life.

There are three states of work commitment that you could face: too much work, not enough work and about the right amount. The last is the best because you can then live a normal life around your work, if you want to. The good thing is that the decision is yours, dependent upon what you wish to achieve in being freelance.

If you have too much work, you will work all the hours God sends. This will be tiring and fulfilling at the same time, but you may have to sacrifice time spent with family and friends. You may find that you don't pull your weight around the house, which could cause tensions with those you live with. If you live alone, who's going to do the domestic chores? Everybody will 'cut you some slack' when you are busy and have deadlines to meet, but if it becomes a way of life to work all the time, something has to give in the end. It could be your relationships or your health – or your business, as your work might begin to deteriorate.

If you have too little work, you may become anxious or even depressed, which could also have disastrous effects on family and friends. You may have the time to spend with them, but you could be such miserable company that nobody really wants to be with you.

Even if you don't go to the extremes when you have little work, what are you going to do with the free time? We looked at the things you can do from a business perspective yesterday. From a personal perspective, what could you be doing with your time? Remember, there's a good chance that your friends will be at work, so you can't fill your day with them.

The best thing to achieve is a sense of balance between work and personal life, which takes into account the highs and lows of your workload.

Time management and discipline

Meeting deadlines and getting the work done provides its own discipline. If you upset clients or miss deadlines, you will end up not having too much repeat business from them. Even so, it is difficult to sustain long periods of 'burning the candle at both ends', both physically and mentally. Not only that, but if you push yourself too much you will find that the quality and speed of your work will drop off.

Rest and relaxation is important, even during the busiest periods, as it enables you to keep performing to the best of your ability. It also has the advantage of avoiding negative impacts on your life such as disgruntled and unsupportive family and friends, which in turn could add to your tensions.

It is vital to manage your time and discipline yourself. Time management and discipline should be employed not just for business and work but also for your personal life as well. Try to keep involved in hobbies and activities. It is a good idea to set aside one day of the week where you do not do any work at all but concentrate on spending time with people.

If you work from home, discipline yourself to take time out. I often find that when my wife comes in from work, one of my first questions is, 'What do you want to do this evening?' What this really means is, 'I want to do something, or go somewhere', because I have been indoors all day. On the other hand, she has been out at work and wants to relax at home. Having experienced tensions at first, we are now sensitive to the situation and strike a balance.

The same sensitivity needs to be employed with regard to holidays. If possible, plan to have a holiday. Even if you are unable to go away, set aside the time as a holiday and inform your clients that you will be on holiday, so that they don't expect you to be at the end of the phone or fax. This also provides a good excuse to contact your clients and ask if they have any work for you to do just before, or after, your holiday; this can prove to be profitable. If you stay at home for your holiday, try to do things and go out; after all, you spend the rest of the year at home.

Sickness and back-up

We have covered sickness previously by emphasising the need to be prepared financially. However, sickness presents some other problems. When you are sick, you can't work. This means that you cannot earn money, but you can be insured against this. More importantly, though, if you are sick and cannot work, it means that you could be letting your clients down.

If your type of work is made up of one-off jobs, then it is not so much of a problem, as your obligation is to finish the job on hand. If your work is made up of long-term contracts or retainers, then if you are sick you will not be able to fulfil your obligations. You will then lose that business and probably the goodwill of your client. Therefore, it is worth planning for a back-up, if possible. You may need somebody who will be available to take over your work should anything untoward happen. This could be a friend, or even a competitor!

An example of the need for back-up comes from my own wedding day. A couple of days before my wedding day, the photographer phoned up and said that they would not be at our wedding because of a death in their family. They did not offer us an alternative photographer, recommend a friend or arrange for another photographer to cover for them. Whilst their situation was very sad, it also meant that we did not have a photographer, and therefore no wedding photographs. The net result for the photographer is not only my lost business but also the bad word of mouth which will have filtered into the market.

Research has shown that on average, a satisfied customer tells two to three people about how happy they are with a product or service, while a dissatisfied customer tells at least ten people how unhappy they are. Word-of-mouth recommendations are great, but word-of-mouth denunciations are a disaster!

The need for back-up also applies to having a holiday or taking time off. It can also be a positive factor in attracting business. Being able to cover the situation all the time allows you to pitch for contract and retainer work. Which brings us to the future...

The future

It is really beyond the remit of this book to look too far ahead into the future; we are concerned primarily with the *beginning* of your freelance career. Also, the future is very much in your hands: are you primarily concerned to be just an individual freelancer, or are you planning on starting out as an individual with a view to growing into a business in the long term? Whatever your personal ambitions you do need to keep an eye on the future. Expansion and growth is up to you and your circumstances, but it is vital that you don't stand still. The business world is a dynamic and constantly changing environment, and as a supplier to that world you also need to be able to change. Bearing in mind what business you are in will help you to respond to changes.

Responding to changes may also require capital. It is probably not enough just to earn enough money to live on. You will need to earn and save more. There will come a time when you need to spend more than you are currently earning on equipment or extra marketing activity. You may need to buy a new car, move house, rent an office, or go on a business trip. Although you can't plan for that day, you *can* save for it. Having the money to reinvest in your business will help you run it smoothly and avoid any nasty surprises that the future may throw at you.

Summary

Today we have looked at some of the effects that going freelance will have on your life. There will undoubtedly be more and different things that will occur that we haven't covered, due to your own unique situation and position. Having tried to look holistically at the way that being a freelancer interacts with your normal life, you should now be in a position to work through whatever your new life will bring you, whether positive or negative.

The freelance audit

Assessing what going freelance means to you

1 Good things	2 Bad things
3 Important matters	4 Unimportant matters

When you have thought about the 'freelance decision' write your feelings in the relevant box above. Use the grid to help you generate more responses and clarify your thoughts. How many comments are in each box? Your primary reasons should be in Boxes 1 and 3. Of the points you have written in Box 2, what can you do about them to turn them into positives or make them less important? Your aim should be to plan your freelance decision so as to clear Box 2 of entries, if possible.

The main points

Today we will be recapping exactly what it means to go freelance. It is a unique and exciting opportunity to do your own thing and fulfil your own destiny. You will be presented with challenges and opportunities, but you will also meet some anxious moments and pitfalls along the way. The more time and effort you can put into preparing for the day that you go freelance, the more smoothly it will go: you will ease some of the pain and problems that may assail you, thus enabling you not only to do more work but to actually enjoy yourself as well.

This chapter presents you with action checklists to make sure that you haven't forgotten anything. I would recommend that you really do work through these checklists. They will focus your thinking and preparation, and may be the foundation for a business plan, should you have to prepare and submit one to a bank. A business plan is essentially a document that takes the following factors into account:

- The business idea
- The relationship between the idea and the market – is the idea well-thought-out, based on research and viable?
- The investment needed in the business to make the idea work
- The return on that investment

Normally, a business plan is produced if finance from a bank is required. The following checklists will help you start to formulate not only a business plan but also a greater understanding of your own business and its potential for success.

Action checklist 1

Personal
Please tick those of the following that are relevant to you.

_____   I am ready to be freelance and work for myself.

_____   I know that I have a good idea and the right approach and can make it work.

_____   I understand all the pros and cons of going freelance, and am able to cope with them.

_____   I am more excited than anxious.

_____   I have to give it a go, and will not be able to live with myself wondering, 'What if?'

_____   I have discussed it with my family and friends, and they are supportive.

If you have ticked all of these, you are ready to go freelance.

Action checklist 2

Me and my business
Fill in the following.

My skills are:

My experience is:

My business is:

My strengths are:

My weaknesses are:

My worries are:

During my first lull in work, I am going to:

My back-up if I am unable to work is:

Action checklist 3

My market
Fill out the following.

My primary market is:

The benefits I can offer to my market are:

My three main competitors are:

Their strengths are:

Their weaknesses are:

The reasons why my potential customers should employ me (it is good to get your sales pitch worked out; and it should be flexible enough to be adapted to different types of customer):

The first and best ten people that I can contact are:

1 _____   Tel. _____

2 _____   Tel. _____

3 _____   Tel. _____

4 _____   Tel. _____

5 _____   Tel. _____

6 _____   Tel. _____

7 _____   Tel. _____

8 _____   Tel. _____

9 _____   Tel. _____

10 _____   Tel. _____

Action checklist 4

Money
My annual salary is £_____

My current hourly rate is £_____

My domestic outgoings, per month, are £_____

My anticipated business outgoings, per month, are £_____

I need to earn, per month, £_____

Look back to Monday (Chapter 2). How much equipment do you need and how much will it cost?   £_____

I need to buy (list items and costs):

My projected income, month by month, for the next
12 months is:

Month 1:   £_____

Month 2:   £_____

Month 3:   £_____

Month 4:   £_____

Month 5:   £_____

Month 6:   £_____

Month 7:   £_____

Month 8:   £_____

Month 9:   £_____

Month 10:   £_____

Month 11:   £_____

Month 12:   £_____

My projected outgoings, month by month, for the next 12 months are:

Month 1:   £_____

Month 2:   £_____

Month 3:   £_____

Month 4:   £_____

Month 5:   £_____

Month 6:   £_____

Month 7:   £_____

Month 8:   £_____

Month 9:   £_____

Month 10:   £_____

Month 11:   £_____

Month 12:   £_____

Action checklist 5

Things to do
Below is a list of the things that you need to investigate and
sort out. Tick them as you do them.

_____ Find an accountant and begin my account-keeping

_____ Tell the Inland Revenue that I am self-employed

_____ Contact the Department of Social Security about my
National Insurance contributions

_____ Open a separate bank account

_____ Open a separate savings account for my tax money

_____ Contact HM Excise and Customs about VAT
registration, if I think I will need, or want, to be
registered

_____ Find an independent financial advisor (IFA) and
find out about pensions, income-protection
insurance and professional indemnity insurance

_____ Upgrade my home and car insurance to cover me
for business

_____ Find a solicitor if I need to form a limited liability
company or partnership with somebody

_____ Talk to a bank about funding and business plans,
should I need to

Action checklist 6

The future

I have decided to go freelance on _____

GOOD LUCK!

Further *Successful Business in a Week* **titles all at £6.99.** A complete listing of all titles can be obtained from Katie Ingram on 0171 873 6261.

All Hodder & Stoughton books are available from your local bookshop or can be ordered direct from the publisher. Just tick the titles you want and fill in the form below. Prices and availability subject to change without notice.

To: Hodder & Stoughton Ltd, Cash Sales Department, Bookpoint, 39 Milton Park, Abingdon, Oxon, OX14 4TD. If you have a credit card you may order by telephone – 01235 400414.

E-mail address: orders@bookpoint.co.uk

Please enclose a cheque or postal order made payable to Bookpoint Ltd to the value of the cover price and allow the following for postage and packaging:

UK & BFPO: £1.00 for the first book, 50p for the second book and 30p for each additional book ordered up to a maximum charge of £3.00.

OVERSEAS & EIRE: £2.00 for the first book, £1.00 for the second book and 50p for each additional book.

Name: ....

Address: ....

....

If you would prefer to pay by credit card, please complete:

Please debit my Visa/Mastercard/Diner's Card/American Express (delete as appropriate) card no:

❏ ❏ ❏ ❏ ❏ ❏ ❏ ❏ ❏ ❏ ❏ ❏ ❏ ❏ ❏ ❏

Signature .... Expiry Date ....